GOD SAID "IT IS GOOD!"

GENESIS 1:1-27 ILLUSTRATED

JOHNNIE MAE MABERRY

WestBow Press books may be ordered through booksellers or by contacting:

WestBow Press
A Division of Thomas Nelson & Zondervan
1663 Liberty Drive
Bloomington, IN 47403
www.westbowpress.com
844-714-3454

Scripture taken from the King James Version of the Bible.

ISBN: 978-1-6642-5232-5 (sc)
ISBN: 978-1-6642-5233-2 (e)

Library of Congress Control Number: 2021924922

Print information available on the last page.

WestBow Press rev. date: 06/07/2022

WESTBOW
PRESS®
A DIVISION OF THOMAS NELSON
& ZONDERVAN

ଔ

To my children and grandchildren, may they
always know and believe they are created
in the image of GOD. And, so are you.

GOD SAID "IT IS GOOD!" by editor
servant/artist Johnnie Mae Maberry

THE MASTER ARTIST, THE MIRACLE WORKER, THE POWER GREATER THAN ANY POWER WE COULD EVER IMAGINE BEGAN THE STORY OF CREATION. GOD SPOKE THE WORD AND ALL OF CREATION BEGAN.

THIS BOOK IS A VISUAL JOURNEY INSPIRED BY GOD'S HOLY WORDS IN GENESIS 1: 1-27. THE MASTER ARTIST EQUIPPED WITH HIS TOOLS OF LINES, SHAPES, COLOR, VALUES, SPACE, AND TEXTURES FORMED THE UNIVERSE AND GAVE US EACH AN OPPORTUNITY TO SHARE THE SPACE. THIS BOOK IS AN ILLUSTRATION OF THE MOVEMENTS, RHYTHM, HARMONIES, REPETITION, BALANCE, AND SYNCHRONIZATION THAT I EXPERIENCED WHILE READING GENESIS 1: 1-27.

IF EVERYONE COULD EXPERIENCE THE MAGIC AND DYNAMICS OF ALL THAT HAPPENED DURING CREATION, THE FULL IMPACT OF BEING MADE IN THE IMAGE OF OUR AMAZING, CREATIVE, EXCITING, ALL POWERFUL GOD REVEALS HOW SPECIAL WE ALL ARE.

In the beginning God created the Heavens and the earth

Gen. 1:1, KJV

4

THE EARTH WAS WITHOUT FORM, AND VOID*; AND DARKNESS WAS UPON THE FACE OF THE DEEP. AND THE SPIRIT OF GOD MOVED UPON THE FACE OF THE WATERS.

(Gen. 1:2, KJV)

THERE
WAS
NOTHING
BUT
DARKNESS

THEN GOD SAID,
"LET THERE BE LIGHT":

(Gen. 1:3a, KJV)

AND

THERE

WAS

LIGHT

AND GOD SAW THE LIGHT,
THAT IT WAS GOOD;

(Gen. 1:4a,KJV)

"...AND GOD DIVIDED* THE LIGHT FROM THE DARKNESS.

(Gen. 1:4b, KJV)

GOD CALLED
THE LIGHT DAY,
AND THE
DARKNESS
HE CALLED NIGHT.
AND THE EVENING
AND THE MORNING

WERE THE FIRST DAY.

(Gen. 1:5, KJV)

LIGHT BECAME DAY AND
DARKNESS BECAME NIGHT

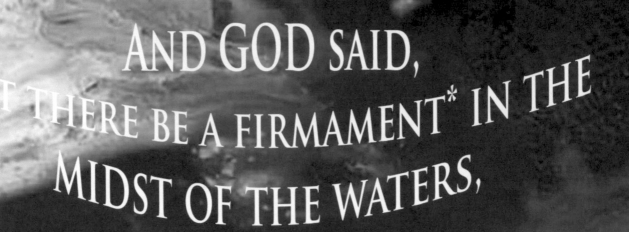

AND GOD SAID,
"LET THERE BE A FIRMAMENT* IN THE
MIDST OF THE WATERS,

AND LET IT DIVIDE THE WATERS FROM THE WATERS"

AND GOD MADE THE FIRMAMENT,
AND DIVIDED THE WATERS
WHICH WERE UNDER THE FIRMAMENT
FROM THE WATERS
WHICH WERE ABOVE THE FIRMAMENT;
AND IT WAS SO.
AND GOD CALLED THE FIRMAMENT HEAVEN.

AND THE EVENING AND THE MORNING
WERE THE SECOND DAY.

(Gen. 1:7-8, KJV)

AND GOD SAID,

"LET THE WATERS UNDER THE HEAVENS BE GATHERED TOGETHER INTO ONE PLACE,

(Gen. 1:9, KJV)

AND LET THE DRY LAND APPEAR";
AND IT WAS SO.

AND GOD CALLED
THE DRY LAND
EARTH,
AND THE GATHERING TOGETHER
OF THE WATERS
HE CALLED SEAS.

AND GOD SAW
THAT IT WAS GOOD.

(Gen. 1:10b, KJV)

15

AND GOD SAID,

"LET THE EARTH BRING FORTH* GRASS,
THE HERB THAT YIELDING SEED,
AND THE FRUIT TREE THAT YIELDING FRUIT
AFTER HIS KIND, WHOSE
SEED IS IN ITSELF, UPON THE EARTH":
AND IT WAS SO.

(Gen. 1:11, KJV)

AND THE EARTH BROUGHT FORTH GRASS,
THE HERB THAT YIELDING SEED AFTER
HIS KIND, AND THE TREE YIELDING FRUIT,
WHOSE SEED WAS IN ITSELF AFTER

HIS KIND:

(Gen. 1:12a, KJV)

AND GOD SAW THAT IT WAS GOOD

AND THE EVENING AND THE MORNING
WERE THE THIRD DAY.
(Gen. 1:12b-13, KJV)

And GOD said, "Let there be lights in the firmament of the heaven to divide the day from the night; and let them be for signs, and for seasons, and for days, and years: (Gen. 1:14, KJV).

GOD MADE THE SUN AND THE SEASONS

AND LET THEM BE FOR LIGHTS IN THE FIRMAMENT OF THE HEAVEN TO GIVE LIGHT UPON THE EARTH": AND IT WAS SO.

(Gen. 1:15, KJV)

AND GOD MADE TWO GREAT LIGHTS; THE GREATER LIGHT TO RULE THE DAY, AND THE LESSER LIGHT TO RULE THE NIGHT:

HE MADE THE STARS ALSO. AND GOD SET THEM IN THE FIRMAMENT OF THE HEAVEN TO GIVE LIGHT ON THE EARTH. AND TO RULE OVER THE DAY AND OVER THE NIGHT, AND TO DIVIDE THE LIGHT FROM THE DARKNESS.

(Gen. 1:16-18a, KJV)

GOD DIVIDED
THE DAY FROM NIGHT

AND GOD SAW THAT
IT WAS GOOD.
AND THE EVENING AND
THE MORNING WERE THE
FOURTH DAY.

(Gen 1:18b-19, KJV)

AND GOD SAID, "LET THE WATERS BRING FORTH ABUNDANTLY* THE MOVING CREATURE THAT HATH LIFE, AND FOWL THAT MAY FLY ABOVE THE EARTH IN THE OPEN FIRMAMENT OF THE HEAVEN.

(Gen. 1:20, KJV)

23

AND GOD CREATED GREAT WHALES, AND EVERY LIVING CREATURE THAT MOVETH*, WHICH THE WATERS BROUGHT FORTH ABUNDANTLY, AFTER THEIR KIND,

(Gen. 1:21a, KJV)

...AND EVERY WINGED FOWL

AFTER HIS KIND.

AND GOD SAW THAT

IT WAS GOOD.

(Gen. 1:21b, KJV)

GOD MADE THE BIRDS

*AND GOD BLESSED THEM, SAYING,
"BE FRUITFUL AND MULTIPLY*, AND FILL THE WATERS
IN THE SEAS, AND LET FOWL* MULTIPLY
IN THE EARTH".*

AND THE EVENING
AND THE MORNING WERE THE
FIFTH DAY.

(Gen. 1:22-23, KJV)

AND GOD SAID, "LET THE EARTH BRING FORTH THE LIVING CREATURE ACCORDING TO HIS KIND*, CATTLE, AND CREEPING* THING, AND BEAST* OF THE EARTH AFTER HIS KIND":

AND IT WAS SO.

(Gen 1:24, KJV)

AND GOD MADE THE BEAST OF THE EARTH
AFTER HIS KIND, AND CATTLE
AFTER THEIR KIND,

AND EVERY THING
THAT CREEPETH UPON THE EARTH
AFTER HIS KIND:

AND GOD SAW THAT
IT WAS GOOD.
GOD MADE ALL THE ANIMALS
ON EARTH
(Gen. 1:25, KJV)

AND GOD SAID, "LET US MAKE MAN
IN OUR IMAGE*, AFTER
OUR LIKENESS*: AND LET THEM
HAVE DOMINION OVER THE
FISH OF THE SEA, OVER THE
FOWLS OF THE AIR,

AND OVER THE CATTLE, AND OVER
ALL THE EARTH AND OVER
EVERY CREEPING THING THAT
CREEPETH ON THE EARTH"

(Gen. 1:26, KJV)

SO GOD CREATED MAN IN HIS OWN IMAGE;

IN THE IMAGE OF GOD HE CREATED HIM;
MALE AND FEMALE HE CREATED THEM.

And GOD said Let us make man in our image after our likeness. So GOD created a man in His image, in the image of GOD created He him; male and female Created He them (Gen. 1:26-27))

LOOK INTO A MIRROR

(Gen. 1:27, KJV)

LOVE
Peace
Courage
GOODNESS
HOLY
Kindness
TRUTH
Gratitude
RIGHTEOUS
TRUST
No Fear
No Fear
FORGIVENESS
GRACE
Strong
Honor
Patience
COMPASSION
FAITH
Merciful
JOY
HOPE

AND GOD SAW EVERYTHING THAT HE MADE,
AND, BEHOLD, IT WAS VERY GOOD.
(Gen 1:31, KJV)

WE ARE MADE IN THE IMAGE OF A GOOD GOD,
CREATED TO BE GOOD AND DO GOOD.
WE EACH HAVE A SHARE IN ALL THE GOODNESS
WHICH INCLUDES LOVE, JOY, PEACE,
AND KINDNESS THAT IS WITHIN

THE CREATOR.

LET US BE THE GOOD
GOD HAS CREATED.
LOVE ONE ANOTHER AS
GOD LOVES US. AMEN

Clarification of in text Terms and phases:

1. Abundant- Many, a lot of something
2. "after their kind/his kind"-animals, plants, and living things of the same species
3. "after our likeness"- to look, act or be like someone else
4. "beast of the earth"- animals of the earth
5. "bring forth"- to be filled with; to be included in a certain environment
6. Creatures-animals
7. Creepeth-same as creeps, able to physically move
8. Divide- separate, split into
9. Firmament- like clouds, smoke, steam
10. Fowl- birds, things with wings/feathers
11. Good- all things made by GOD
12. Hath- has or had
13. Herb- vegetables and spices
14. Moveth- moves or moved
15. Multiply- Make more of many times over
16. Void- empty, nothingness

EXHIBIT

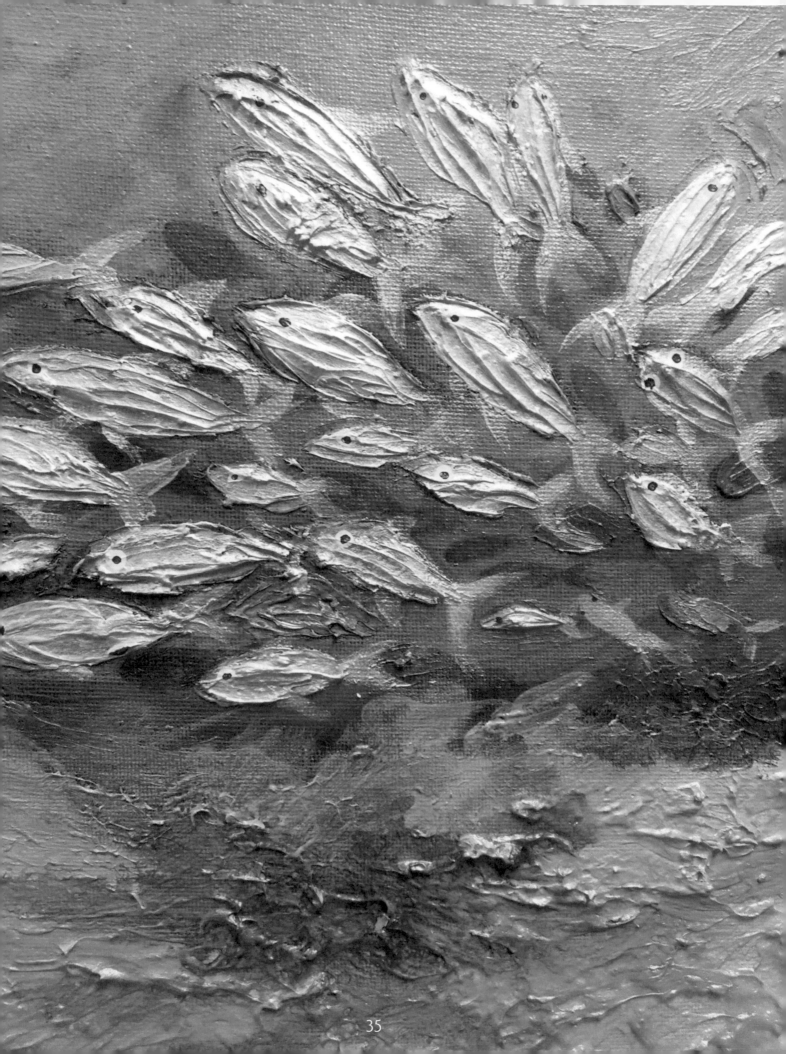